WIDE-ONS

WIDE-ONS

for Tony Harding
hello & good
wishes!
Diane Christian
September 1989

by

Diane Christian

Introduced by Robert Creeley

Synergistic Press, San Francisco

Copyright 1981
by Synergistic Press
3965 Sacramento Street
San Francisco, California 94118

Manufactured in the United States

First Edition

Library of Congress Cataloging in Publication Data

Christian, Diane, 1939–
   Wide-ons.

I. Title.
PS 3553.H726W5   811'.54   81-8979
ISBN 0-912184-00-0   AACR2
ISBN 0-912184-01-9 (pbk.)

WIDE-ONS was set in Goudy Oldstyle, with titles in Goudy Bold,
by Rapid Typographers, San Francisco. Thomson-Shore, Inc., of Dexter,
Michigan printed the book on Glatfelter B-31. It was bound by
John Dekker & Sons, Grand Rapids, Michigan. Ron Sagara designed
the book and its cover. The photographs of Diane Christian on the cover
and page 61 are by Bruce Jackson.

for Bruce Jackson

"his speech is sweet, and he is
altogether desirable"

The Song of Songs

CONTENTS

Robert Creeley's position in the forefront of contemporary American poetry is recognized and secure. When he agreed to write the introduction for this collection by his faculty colleague at the State University of New York at Buffalo, where he is Gray Professor of Poetry & Letters, it was certain that the result would be personal, sensitive and distinctive. It was, reflective of the friendliness and wit which *American Poets Since World War II* notes is present in so much of Creeley's work.

Creeley is especially qualified to introduce this collection for most of the poems in his *For Love* comment on the myriad possibilities of love and friendship and his poems in *Words* speak often of love, friendship and the human body.

The introduction—the poem "For a Big Sister" printed on the facing page—shows why Creeley is a voice spare, powerful and clearly human, an analyst of human relationships who is one of America's greatest living poets.

For A Big Sister

Experience not only teaches--
it moves you on. Hence
the wry fey deftness
of these songs...

Given under seal this 20th
day of December, 1980, in homage
to and respect of The Boss, viz
Diane as in Moon, and Christian
as in Tempers and Trials.

Your friend,

Robert

[i.e., Bright and
Far Shining ...

about the title:

it's meant to be a punning
mostly

somewhat on a lady lib locution
somewhat on desire
a little bit on me.

but not entirely

**To me upon deciding
to leave the convent after 7½ years:**

all done nun

A former to a present nun: reminder

one nice thing
about loving Christ

is you're sure
he isn't screwing
your neighbor

Braless at 30

You can't walk around like that
he said
meaning not braless but firm and fancy

a madras and one bra less later
we strolled the village
hip, and bouncy I

Who'd have imagined that a few bound-up years ago?

poetry is pure

I hate pain
and so build fences
holes to scoot through
silly talk and shores.

I once wrote a poem
about the light & dance & danger
       of the sea
and staying on the shore.

The last lines went:
       "and I was shore and still and dry
       —a boundary to the sea."

That may well, alas,
       be me.

But I do hope for sea.

I wish over and over

I wish over and over
to offer you a poem
which like a fabled sweet small bird
      will sing golden-throated
      the honey and the sun
      you seem and seam for me.
But the bird is bashful stubborn
and the song is slow to rise
and I am plagued with fearful cries
that I shall never bring
sweet honey and warm sun.

Just as our bodies touch
      but turn
the impulse too may burn
      away
      unsung.

I wait a man

I wait a man
to woman for and to
without strain
or having to
kiss softly with my soul at tips
only silent holding soft
I like all parts and a sweet
reserve which can
come and go
stay and play
whatever.

someone willing—wanting better—
to man a little me

what I hate

what I hate
about being a woman
is
waiting

In response to
"The Pill vs. the Springhill Mine Disaster"

for Richard Brautigan and Pope Paul

if my pill saddens you
with thoughts of people perishing inside me

imagine my anguish
at the billions of possible people

you Portnoys
have jerked off

summer & winter

for Angus Fletcher
"There is truth in extremes—keep them." (Blake)

spring and fall continual
are indeed your song
the rhythm
not the line
which does define
a maze
—unwilling
to be ending
to be bending
  save to kiss
  and miss perfections
but ever to away and rise
another goodly frame
to name not game
not spring and fall
  the rhythm
but summer winter bounds
—the arch of line that redefines
  the rhythm
  and the rhyme

I trust you farther than I can spit

I trust you farther than I can spit
not because I know you knight
or feel I'm bright
or trust in old true grit

just because, o, I can spit

Calmly courteous charming cool

Calmly courteous charming cool
I chatter with my aunt and friend
aware
that you
only a chair away
wish to touch and hold me
And the energy all warm in me
flows to you
while my head is turned.

Balm for Hera

I appreciate your position
identify in fact
(and I'm too proud to have your ease of anger
—my world would be as full of bulls as heifers)
Merlin from another time
said there is no comfort
save to "learn something"

for me it's this:
>   balm bombs in the moment
>   but makes poetry in the end

thus we gain one end or another.

I worked you out of heart

I worked you out of heart
at last
and with small grace to spare

out of head too
You're no longer all
and always there.

But as I sit hearing of spooky Dante
o
you linger at my lips.

Why does poetry make me love you?

It is long since

It is long since
excited sap
has swelled my veins
    almost a year
    another fall ago
And I am grateful
    for the rush
    though still
    there is no tree
    for me.

driving first behind

driving first behind
and then before you
      images of trail
      and touch
      engulf me

Light rain falls
on night panes
distrusting moonlight
and afraid
I open my house
to you

sparrow & dove

you told of an omen in your cellar
(where's the sparrow, daddy?)
another in an airport
(that's a dove, sir!)

> curly-headed man
> you laughed and looked and sat
> with only eyes
> like birds restive at strange rest.

Are you bound to be a bird
eagle by damn whatever what the shit?

I confess to libidinous perching
this dove of spirit sighs for Venus broods
—it augurs an old tale
> golden nets
> > peace courting war.

Advice against intent is seemly
Thus:
> sparrow to my dove
> providence, make peace,
> and I'll give sweet reverses
> (a harder war to fly between
> cellars and airports of desire)

why is it

why is it
I am warm
to pleasure you?
   taboo? or dangerous male?
   my own itch for impossibles?
   a common hunger we apprise?

I hardly know you close or far
we reach for syllables and style

Better I concoct you
   than
   find you man

And if I make you poetry
What will you make of me?

halloween

and unholy hopes.
I wait working
wishing
you might come
trick or treat
absolutely

Like the pickaninny gobblers
earlier tonight
I'm greedy, and needy,
black inside.

you know harsh things

you know harsh things
and do not shut your eyes
to your own bawl or crotch or cover

       It gives you a crazy truth
       straight and with compassion

It gives me a crazy wish
to kiss closed a space
your eyes.

either / or or more

we'll either get bored or uncomfortable
you said
it's perfectly clear how it ends
sad alternatives I said
o, it doesn't completely die, you softened,
you redefine relation
o, said I, imitating ingenuous o-maker you.
I don't believe the bind though
although
I know
we both fear truth is ending.
You, man, precipitate; I, woman, wait
—separation and its staying
you're either, I or
but there is also more

My man Blake says

My man Blake says
"Sooner murder an infant in its cradle
than nurse unacted desires"

So I don't desire you
won't say it feel it think it
will trade agape for eros
and desire to displace you
with the first perfectly lovable man
who copes into me

words & pictures

traditionally I give flesh
you form
Yet I gave words and you two gulls
flying wordlessly across my desk

mute in a grey field
one arches gently
the other dips and covers right

the wings are like
the tops of hearts
the bodies like male sex

They do not strain.
pictura poesis
a spare and lovely word

to circle stay

to circle stay
touch relay
to let me hide in him.

All this may be a myth
I've often thought it
some parent compensation or escape

"romantic hokey" says a friend of mine
ok
and yet

because of you
        dreams spring

"What does paradise do for you?"

"What does paradise do for you?
I mean," he said
"does all that pleasure turn you on?"

hello to a lover*

*if a label's needed

sweet roots of milk and honey
passion's fruits are pale

The sandpipers at Carmel were very nice

The sandpipers at Carmel were very nice
you wrote, adding,
     "that's for consolation or ratification, unsure which"

I think of a Taylor-Burton movie—"B"
the pound of the sea and illicit passion
and of John of the Cross
warning the bird can be bound by slimmest thread
and of desire, both kinds.

The sandpipers know neither and are free
ratification of all the sun sea flying
we would do in innocence but cannot in desire
and so dream picture poems of birds.

The looking back does not console
longing embitters, Orpheus fades.

But sandpipers remain free
as dream we.

I wonder

I wonder
if the intimacy I dream
would drown a distance you desire
or the other way around.
Finding out would end this problem.

I wrote:

My favorite thought
is sexy and sensational
no soft light or scene
just you and I
and you plunge
into
me

it's fine

He responded:

"When you write poems about me & you contiguous
They sure are fucken unambiguous."

Valentine's Day

Across the bobbing heads
I see your eyes
and stare hello.
They claim me I think
out of the dancing arms and loins about me
And I want to walk
straight across the room
and into them
to test the rest and restlessness
to live in them a time
It's something new to me
not the passion or the tenderness
(though they are always new)
but the freedom
being there

You spice my life with sweetness

You spice my life with sweetness
ginger peachy jams

I dress simmering for your tongue
I dream talking to your eyes

Last night I had your baby
and waking said
       keep the spices on the shelf
       and find another burner.

Passover 1971

he stayed his sword
at my door
and brought life
like all who've seen the angel of the lord
I hold his night
holy

a decision today

a decision today
in opening May
to find another way
love and say and play
myself
to some other
not you
I

postcard to John Hollander

foreign country here I come
will you have tulips for me?
with windmills I am overrun

Germaine Greer

Germaine Greer
would not be stewed
as I
undone and anxious over you

She would not listen
and twist her neck at every racing engine
carry the phone to the shower
and leave notes on the door

Germaine Greer
would be cool

damn her

who ever are you

who ever are you
sitting in that chair
keeping my eyes closed
asking me what tree I am

Last week

for Dick Donovan

Last week a friend called
in a frenzy of love's splitting

And I, myself so full of you,
I comforted
      saying believe in the dream
      don't diminish defect or despair

Then I wrote a letter saying same
      and girdling my own joy.
The next day my dream was shown defective,
      deflowered in a sentence,
      all the sweetness sickened.
I sobbed three days, burst blood vessels
      in my eyes
      and longed alone for sleep

Today I write my friend again
      saying see you on the sea
      but I still believe it's possible

the friendly girl

the friendly girl
who calls and asks me
about my love
has been his lover
I found out the other day
strange mushroom poison

you who were

you who were
all pleasure
running over
sweet honeycomb of love
are now
all pain
gnawing under
the sweetness of all life

which is to show
you never know

worm of desire be damned

worm of desire be damned
who gave you life
to ravish every hour
with hunger for a rose
a bed a rapture
who gave you leave
to ravage every sweetness
unto rot

what kind of man do you want? he asked

very smart
very sexy
very trusty too, I answered

and how have you fared? said he

one was smart and fairly trusty, failed in passion
two was only passion though he tried
three seemed everything then showed untrusty

others appeared in assorted mixes,
for various reasons untried

my next idea is to raise the fare

pleasant it is to be publicly wise

The night before you left

The night before you left
we went wild in each other
silently slapping thighs
roaming pain and pressure
before predictable ease.
After which without a word
we sank still wrapped
into deep sleep.

Next day we parted politely
though our breath was broken.
Old harsh mountains shadowed
a strange and frothy space.

I intend to get it

I intend to get it
I said (to you)
meaning practice at sucking the sweet male cock
meaning more a manifesto
that your ever-receding cock your
       occasionally errant cock
       wasn't the sole sweet in the universe
meaning
       don't go.

I / love / you / lengthily

I
  love
    you
      lengthily
up and down
soft flesh and hard
sweet black curls
and curving under thigh
silent space inside and
round again
an endless place
sea forest sky blaze
horizon world of you

backgrounds

we are different they note
refining racy and rigorous pasts
you the rogue and I the virgin

I might remark
I was harlot in heart
and you a saint

I might cite Yeats:
artist and saint choose
circumference and center
tracing the same circle

we meet, my love,
not by such opposites
nor even by analogy
but both and oneful
finding free
a foreground, we.

you're like a tropical garden he wrote

you're like a tropical garden he wrote
lush and moist and self-possessed
with secret parts, dark cools

the garden is yours say I
beloved and beautiful man
paradise regained

The poet

Diane Christian was born in New York City on the
last day of the Thirties. Her father remarks that she was a
sweeping deduction at birth but overcompensated quickly.
She grew up in Rochester, N.Y., where she moved at four.
She was educated there by the sisters of St. Joseph whose
community she joined after college.

Her youth was enhanced by the fib to best friends that she
was Wonder Woman. But "St. Thérèse failed to deliver
the costume" and lost thereby her fervent cultist, and the
myth dwindled. Diane now understands that entering
the convent was as much journeying to Paradise Island, a
sanctuary where women are powerful and fine Amazons, as
it was answering the call of Christ to perfection.

She took an MA and PhD at The Johns Hopkins
University. Her dissertation was on William Blake whom she
credits with wrestling her from the convent. She taught
as a sister and a secular at Nazareth University in Rochester
and then went to The State University of New York at
Buffalo where she presently is an Associate Professor of
English. One of her courses there is the popular "Bible
as Literature."

At Buffalo she met Bruce Jackson with whom she co-
authored *Death Row* and co-produced and directed the
documentary movie of the same title. They married in 1973
and she "inherited three terrific children."

She is now doing a book and a film, funded by the National
Endowment for the Humanities, on ex-nuns. Both are
called *Out of Order*. She also is finishing her book on Blake
and the body. An executive director of Documentary
Research, Inc., a Buffalo-based not-for-profit organization
producing documentaries in various media, she likes purple.

WIDE-ONS is her first published book of poems. She says
the next will be *Love and War*.

Other titles from SYNERGISTIC PRESS

Clancy, Judith. LAST LOOK AT THE OLD MET. A personal last portrait, in drawings and text, of the old Metropolitan Opera House. 54 pages. Gold-stamped Kivar over boards. ISBN 0-912184-03-7. $ 5.95
> "...charming pen and ink line drawings of the inside of the Old Met during its last few days...Judith Clancy, who drew them, writes as beguilingly about herself as she draws."
> Mary Campbell, ASSOCIATED PRESS

Fisher, M.F.K. and Clancy, Judith. NOT A STATION BUT A PLACE. Mrs. Fisher's text memories of the Gare de Lyon in Paris and its magnificent Train Bleu restaurant introduce Ms. Clancy's drawings and collages. 72 pages. Gold-stamped Kivar over boards.
ISBN 0-912184-03-3. $ 9.95
Quality softcover. ISBN 0-912184-03-1.   5.95
> "Taken together, prose and pictures accurately and movingly evoke what it was (and is) like to spend time, eating and awaiting a train, in this lovely old station." David Shaw, LOS ANGELES TIMES